Storm
Survivors

STORM SURVIVORS

William A. Jordan

Atlanta, Georgia

Storm Survivors

Published in 2012 by   Pure Publishing, LLC

P O Box 1493

Fairburn, GA 30213.

For more information about Pure Publishing, visit our web site at
www.purepublishingllc.com.

Library of Congress Cataloging-in-Publications-Data

Unless otherwise indicated, Scripture quotations are from the
Amplified or King James Version of the Holy Bible. (Via
Biblegateway.com) All rights reserved.

Cover Design: Sammy Blackmon

Printed in the United States of America

10 9 8 7 6 5 4 3 2 1

ISBN: 0-615-74509-1

William A. Jordan

Acknowledgements

The idea of storm survivors was germinated in council and conversations with parishioners of my congregation who were in the midst of calamites. Dr. A. Louis Patterson, Jr. said preachers should mirror the moment and I took his wise council and the Lord gave birth to this project.

I'm grateful to my wife, Nikki, and my children, Jeff Taylor and Amiya Elizabeth, for their love and support.

I bless the Lord for my mother, Ollie Jean Jordan-Monk, for her love, support and prayers.

I want to thank the members of the Lyons Unity Church for challenging me to become a better pastor and preacher.

I pay homage to my mentors and heroes in the faith, Dr. Joe Samuel Ratliff and Dr. Ralph Douglas West, for their council and support.

Special thanks to my team at Pure Publishing, LLC! You all are the best and a gift to the body of Christ.

My final and most profound thanks goes to GOD, my Father, CHRIST, my Savior, and my blessed comforter; who guided me in this endeavor that will bless the lives of countless storm survivors.

Praise be unto GOD!

CONTENTS

Acknowledgments

Introduction

1   No One Is Exempt From Trouble   3

2   Unexpected Storms   15

3   You're Not Under Attack--You're Tired   25

4   Lord Help Me Survive The Storm I Created   37

5   Bend Don't Break   45

6   God Has Not Forgotten About You   53

7   You're Almost There--Don't Give Up   61

8   You Will Survive   67

9   The Perfect Storm   73

About the Author

Trouble has no respect of persons.

It matters not a person's age, race, religion, or creed; trouble is everywhere you go. You can be as young as sixteen year old Gabrielle Douglas—the talented, African-American 2012 Olympian—or as old as the individual who is in the evening of their life; if it hasn't already, trouble will find you. I can assure you that before you kiss your loved ones for the last time; before your eyes get weary and close never to open again; you will have an experience with trouble. But, as the old church mothers would often say, "Trouble don't last always." Beloved, I can say with surety that trouble will come but I can also assure you that it doesn't come to stay.

In the church gamut, we refer to trouble as storms. However, in the natural realm, we can usually pinpoint a storm's cause, arrival, and duration. But, in the spiritual realm, storms do not always need a reason to transpire. They come when they want to and seemingly stay far longer than any of us would care for them to. It has been said that storms come to make you stronger. I can't really point you towards a Biblical reference that proves that; however, I can tell you (and I'm sure you can attest to this) that after you have been through a storm you are never the same.

As much as I would love to say my life has coasted these some thirty-eight years on the smooth highway of peaceful bliss, I can't. In the words of Langston Hughes, "Life for me ain't been no crystal stare." As blessed as I am, as saved as I am, and as much as I love the Lord, I have had my fair share of disdain, discomfort, and disappointment. There have been many nights when my eyes refused to close due to the nagging voice of worry and the taunting cries of distress. There were days when my tears kept my face company, and my mind threatened to pack up its mental stability and give way to insanity. But through it all, and in spite of it all, I am still here. I lived to tell the story, and write this book, of how I weathered the many tumultuous storms of life. I lived so that I could share with others how to not just speak to the storm and pray for it to cease, but how to survive it once you realize you have no other choice but to endure it.

Often times in church, we base how spiritually mature we are on the manner in which we are able to navigate through life's storms. In this book, you will not discover a measuring guide that will specifically indicate where one stands on the spiritual Richter scale for dealing with trouble. You will not find a list that details what qualifies you for the Christian of the Year Award if you ride out each storm with no complaints. Because the truth is, sometimes, trouble will have you feeling as though you are not spiritual at all. Trouble will cause you to sometimes question the very faith that has been the bedrock of your relationship with Christ.

Trouble will cause you to wage war with yourself, resulting in a battle worse than any battle you could ever have with your enemy. See, storms leave damage and often times it's not the damage that can be seen with the human eye. Sometimes, the emotional damage of a storm is far greater than any physical damage that can be done. You can replace things, but it is not always the easiest feat to recover from a heart and soul wound caused by a storm. So, my goal is not to demean, degrade, or dehumanize one for having adverse physical reactions to a spiritual action; but, instead, my objective is to inspire those who are currently experiencing storms and don't know what to do. Or maybe you know what to do but lack the strength and ability to do it.

It is my prayer that by the end of this book you will not necessarily appreciate the storms that come, but appreciate the lessons you learn in them. No, the words in this book will not lead to the promise of you liking what you are left with after the storm has come and gone; but, I hope to challenge you to be eternally grateful for what you did NOT lose in the wind and the rain...you.

William A. Jordan

Chapter One

~

No One Is Exempt From Trouble

D o you remember the day you got saved? The day you took that walk that seemed to last an eternity down the church's aisle to stand before the Pastor and declare that Jesus Christ was your personal Savior? I am pretty sure that day seems like a distant memory until you force yourself to remember. However, I can almost guarantee that most of you reading this were probably under the impression that when you made that decision everything in your life would be as sweet as a Georgia peach or as rosy as a newborn baby's cheek. But, tell me, how long was it before you figured out that was not the case? How long did it take for you to get angry with the Lord for allowing your life to be in shambles AFTER you'd made him Lord over it? If we tell the truth, we have all had those days when we ponder if life was better before we got saved; before we started trying to do the "right thing." You are probably nodding your head in agreement because you know sometimes life seems to actually get worse when you make up your mind to live for Jesus.

One of the first things I want to address in this book is this: You are not a bad Christian just because you experience storms—or periods in your life that are unfavorable. Going through a bad time does not always mean you have done something wrong, God is not pleased, or you are not spiritually judicious. Many leaders in the modern day church, in the 'name it-claim it' era, have in my opinion misled people into believing that if you experience trials and tribulations, then perhaps your faith is not where it needs to be. That is the furthest thing from the truth. There are many biblical examples of great men and women of God who had to endure and press their way through many dark nights and lonely days. Storms are going to come no matter how deeply rooted you are in your faith. And to go one step further, they do not always cease simply because we tell them or want them to. But wouldn't it be great to have the ability to control the storms as we please? How many of us would prevent trouble from happening if we had that much power? How many of us would forgo the lessons that some storms teach us if we had the opportunity to bypass them? If nobody else did, I know I would. If I had my way, I would live in heaven on Earth every single day. Every day would be Sunday, and Sabbath would have no end. But, the reality is, we can't at will press a stop button to cease trouble.

I am convinced that *some* storms come to:

1) Expose our weaknesses

2) Reveal our strengths

3) Reveal our character

I recall vividly the aftermath of Hurricane Katrina. As if the loss of property and priceless possessions were not devastating enough, what pulled on the strings of most Americans hearts were the slow rescue efforts of the government. It was painstakingly difficult to sit in paralytic fashion as we witnessed a mass amount of people misplaced, drenched and cloaked in hurricane soaked clothing, practically pleading for someone, anyone, to save them. Sadly, many people were not rescued—many did not survive the storm.

One of the first things people do in the midst of tragedies is search for outlets to place the blame and I must say that sometimes that's needed. So customary to the norm, as the nation watched the news unfold about the storm's damage, slowly information about the defective levees was revealed. It was discovered that the levees had been broken, but worse, they could have been replaced prior to the appearing of the storm. Herein is also a reflection of point number one that was mentioned above. Hurricane Katrina had simultaneously exposed the weakness of both the government and the levees.

Isn't that how it is? Isn't it easy to reminisce over some instances that have occurred in your life and see where some things could have been done differently? Often times it takes a storm to help us deal with some things we would otherwise ignore. I think it is safe to assume if the storm had not occurred those levees would not have been repaired and we would not know that FEMA's response time to severe national disasters was less than par. The recent Superstorm, Sandy, was the country's first opportunity to show if a lesson had been learned. Within hours FEMA was on the scene, and unlike the eight days it took President Bush to arrive to New Orleans where Katrina struck; President Obama was in the New York area the following day after Sandy made her historic landfall appearance. Some attributed President Obama's response time to an election year political gesture, but I tend to think that it would have been an outcry across the homeland if there was a repeat action of what occurred during Katrina.

So when can you say was the last time your storm showed you? When was the last time you looked into the mirror that was attached to the storm's wave and saw yourself? In everything that we go through, there is something to be learned. Knowledge to be applied. Wisdom to be implemented. But, we must first be willing to not always see the storm as a bad thing.

The second point. Storms show us our strengths. Let's be honest. Think back to the last thing you went through. While going through it you probably thought you would not make it out. But, look at you today. Look at what you survived. It is often said, and is true; we don't know our own strength. As a Pastor, a common mistake I see made by many is the comparison of one's ability to weather storms with another. There is no way you can effectively size up your strength with that of another person. A heavy load to you may feel like cotton balls to someone else. That is why I don't worry about keeping up with the Jones', the Smith's, or anyone else for that matter. I don't know what they had to go through to get where they are, and even if I did know, I am almost certain that I would still be in my own corner, minding my own business, weathering my own storms.

Strengths are often revealed through pain. Over the years I've met plenty of people who went through life altering ordeals that propelled them to press for more out of life. It was through their pain that they pushed beyond the walls of comfortableness and familiarity and developed a determination to persevere and become someone great.

Not only is strength revealed through pain, but strength is also *strengthened* through pain. Each time you emerge from a trial that does not kill you, it has only made you stronger. It may not seem like the pain that you are enduring is doing anything but tearing you into pieces bit by bit, but give it some time.

Here's an example.

Have you ever worked out before? I mean really, really worked out to the point that every inch of you seemed to screech in excruciating pain? Did you work out so much until your body felt like it would never forgive you? Can you recall some days when your muscles felt as if they had been set ablaze? Do you remember thinking you would never work out again in your life? If you are one of the ones who stuck with it, you can attest to the fact that even after all of the turmoil you put your body through, after surviving the mornings where you got out of the bed and it felt as if your legs were spaghetti; one day you looked in the mirror and realized that it was worth it. Why was it worth it? Because you got the results you were going for. And we all know that the more you work out, not only the healthier you become, but the stronger you become. So, sometimes, the storms come to make us stronger. It works our faith muscle. It works our patience muscle. It works our resilience muscle. And before it is all said and done, we are the better because of it.

The third point. It reveals our character. Who are you in the times of trouble? Character is often tested in the midst of a tumultuous time. Dictionary.com defines the word character in many ways, but one of the definitions is: *the strength and originality in a person's nature.*

When all hell breaks loose in your life how do you find yourself responding? What is your usual pattern of behavior? Do you take your frustration out on the people in your life? Do you forget that you are a Christian and start to behave in adverse ways? Or do you maintain your composure? Is it in your character to remain focused during waves of trials?

Don't get me wrong. I am in no way suggesting that if you are not wearing a smile on your face 24/7 it means you lack character. If you say the wrong thing or behave the wrong way in the face of conflict it does not mean you are steps away from hell. But, I am asking you to take a mirror and turn it in your direction when things are going wrong. Often times we will discover some things about ourselves that need improving when it comes to how we react to life's storms. Even as a Pastor, I would be lying if I told you my real time response to trouble was immediately picking up my Bible and burying myself in the Word of God. I wish I could tell you that I rush the altar or spend hours on my face seeking God for answers. Sometimes I do; other times I don't. The point is; however you choose to survive your storm is your personal business as long as you don't forsake the essence of who you are. Don't allow life to beat you down so to the point that you lose you in the process. I cannot count the number of times I have seen my children turn into total different individuals when things did not go their way. They aren't always picture images of angelic beings, but their behavior when they don't like something have often made me wonder if they had someone been injected with the seed of Chucky. All of us, from the youngest to the oldest, act out of character sometimes when things don't go our way.

So, the question is posed. How does one maintain their character in the rising waves of trouble? How does one hold on to what is right, reasonable, and relevant in the midst of our darkest seasons? The answer will sound like a cliché but I've found it to be true.

Here it is: Trust God.

Nothing deep but it is one of the most difficult things to do when you are in a storm. It is very difficult to trust God in the dark especially when pain and suffering is violently crashing against the shore of your life. Trusting God means you have faith in His plan for your life even when you cannot see his blueprints. You know in the end you win, even if you are not quite sure the path you will have to take in order to get to the end.

Here are a few of my favorite scriptures on trusting God.

- *Psalm 16:1 (KJV) – Preserve me, O God: for in thee do I put my trust.*
- *Psalm 22:21 (KJV)-For our heart shall rejoice in him, because we have trusted in his holy name.*
- *Psalm 118: 8 (KJV) – It is better to trust in the Lord than to put confidence in man.*
- *Psalm 34:22 (KJV) – The Lord redeemeth the soul of his servants: and none of them that trust Him shall be desolate.*
- *Psalm 62:8 (KJV) – Trust in Him at all times; ye people, pour out your heart before him: God is a refuge for us. Selah.*
- *Psalm 71:5 (KJV) – For thou art my hope, O Lord God: thou are my trust from my youth.*
- *Psalm 91:2 (KJV) – I will say of the Lord, He is my refuge and my fortress: my God, in Him will I trust.*
- *Isaiah 26:4 (KJV) – Trust ye in the Lord forever: for in the Lord Jehovah is everlasting strength.*

My brothers and sisters, what I am trying to convey to you is there will be some things in life you will not understand.

You just have to trust God.

Things won't all the time make sense.

But, you still must trust God.

There will be some storms that occur that will seem to never end.

Still...trust God.

For in trusting God and remembering His promises, you find peace in the midst of the storm.

Trusting God will keep you sane when the thread of sanity is threatening to break.

Trusting God will give you a blessed assurance that no matter how rough it might get, no matter how dismal the sky may look, or how bleak the outcome appears; there is a hope that lies within that reassures us that by and by, when the morning comes, things will get better.

I want to close this chapter out with a true story of survival recorded by CNN reporter, Jennifer Pangyanszki, after Hurricane Katrina in 2005. She reports:

"Trapped inside the darkened, stifling hot attic of her flooded home in New Orleans with her two teenage daughters, Debbie Este watched her own mother die as they waited for help she thought would never come.

For three days, they waited, sweating and stripped

nearly naked because of the 110-degree heat, with no food and running out of water. The rising water reached the attic and threatened the survival of anyone inside the yellow-sided single-story house.

During half the time they were trapped, the body of Debbie's mom, Melissa Harold, 68, who didn't make it through the ordeal, lay lifeless on the attic floor. Debbie and her girls could hear the chum of helicopters overhead, evacuating neighbors near their house on Arts Street. The sound only reminded them that nobody had come to their rescue.

Their own screams for help were unanswered. Fear got the better of Debbie. She felt so hopeless she thought about using painkillers she had with her to end her and her daughter's plight.

"I said nobody's going to come save us up here and I don't wanna die like this, three days laying in this stinky, dirty water," Debbie Este said. "I couldn't take it anymore. We're gonna die, why don't we just end it quicker?"

For the Estes, one family member was left dead and Debbie and her two daughters made it out alive, joining the hundreds of thousands of displaced people. Before their eventual rescue and relocation to a shelter in Baton Rouge, however, the three trapped survivors had to rescue themselves from succumbing to Debbe Este's desperation. Amanda, her daughter, swayed her mother's talk of suicide by talking about her future.

Temperatures climbed with the water level. On the first day, they watched the water reach the fifth ladder step from the top. On the second day, it lapped onto the attic floor.

The family stayed in the back of the attic, not trusting the other side of the floor, which was weaker. There were no windows, or light, just one small air vent. They took off most of the clothes because it was so hot. With no tools, Tiffany and Amanda, the daughters of Debbie, banged against the inside of the roof, hoping someone would hear and come their rescue.

Having to dip their feet inside of the water to stay cool, they had to repeatedly stop their grandmother from trying to swim to get her purse downstairs. By that Monday evening, the 68-year old woman's condition had deteriorated and her daughter and granddaughters knew she was dying. Six months earlier, she had suffered from congestive heart failure. So, a day and a half after climbing into the attic, Melissa Harold, a former newspaper reporter, passed away.

Soon after, the drinking water as gone. By Wednesday, the same water they had to urinate in started filling up the attic. They inched farther and farther back. The, Debbie Este heard a voice from outside. Her brother, Aldo Harold, 50, had arrived by boat with some friends. Debbie had last talked to him by phone briefly three days earlier when the water starting coming into his house about a mile away. In about five minutes, using an ax, Aldo chopped through the black shingles and wood of the roof so the three of them and two dogs could be pulled into the boat. They were pulled into a surreal scene. All they could see was water all around as they emerged from their drowned house. The boat took them to the Save-A-Lot in their neighborhood. Then they rode in the bed of a pickup truck to the University of New Orleans. From there, a helicopter took them to Baton Rouge, where they stayed in a field hospital for one day while Debbie was treated for dehydration.

Debbie grieved the loss of her mother, but now says her girls are all she needs. Her dream now is to live long enough to have grandchildren." –CNN Reporter Jennifer Pangyanszki

You see, just when you think you have it bad, there is always the testimony of someone who has had it worse. For three days the above mentioned people were unable to eat, drink, or sleep. They had no hope of ever being rescued.

But, they were.

They survived.

Chapter Two

~

Unexpected Storms

I t was a cool, crisp, sunny, summer evening and Jonathan Massey and his wife, Sandra, were sitting on the front porch of their country enjoying a cold glass of freshly squeezed homemade lemonade. They silently and peacefully rocked in their matching rocking chairs as they looked over the green terrain with a setting sun in the background. All was not perfect in their world, but all was indeed well. Their two children were successful in their own rights, their grandkids were growing up in healthy, wholesome environments, their 401ks were secure, their bank account was in the positive and other than a few backaches and blurry vision; they were also in pretty good health. And although they were well into their fifties, they still had a vibrant marriage and remained each other's best friend.

Jonathan, a sales rep for a pharmaceutical company, and Sandra, a RN, enjoyed their evening ritual of meeting on the porch to relax and enjoy the flirtatious stroke of the wind against their cheeks. Of all the nearly twenty years they'd been living in their home, they had never experienced a break in, they had never experienced rude, obtrusive neighbors, and they had never experienced any major damage to their home in spite living in a very tornado prone environment.

Until today.

Suddenly, the wind got angry and before long the serene, blissful atmosphere was interrupted by an unexpected tornado that was quickly approaching. Jonathan and Sandra bumped into each other as they scrambled to get inside to safety. Just as they made it to the bathroom to seek shelter in the bathtub, they could hear the windows screaming as they burst into tiny glass pieces. As the storm's fury intensified, fear began to settle into a permanent place in their heart. The reality that they may not survive gripped their minds robbing them of the ability to have the faith that they would. They declared their love for each other and held each other tighter as they prepared for the worst. Seconds later the roof was violently lifted from the home and several seconds after that, the home was jolted from its foundation and they found themselves being hoisted up into the tornado. Mentally giving up, they made their individual peace with God and prepared to die.

After what seemed like an eternity, what was left of the house came to a halt somewhere in the middle of the acreage that was once a beautiful, scenic sight of rolling hills and barreled hay. The loud, boisterous sound of the storm had been replaced with the deafening sound of destruction. It was quiet. But in the midst of the silence there was the faintest sound of two heartbeats. Both Jonathan and Sandra had survived. Their home was destroyed but they were alive.

Let's think about that story. Can you recall any times when you were ambushed by trouble? When something caught you of guard and disrupted your entire life, and as resourceful and accomplished as you are, there was nothing you could do?

I remember an unexpected storm formed in my life back in my late 20's. The day had started like any other day with the exception that on this particular day I had to go to a routine doctor's visit. Sure, I was having a few complications, but nothing was seriously wrong. However, after getting there and being checked it out, I was told that it was a possibility I had prostate cancer. Although it turned out to be a negative report, I remember the many sleepless nights I endured due to the antagonizing mental torture that would arrest any positive thoughts I had. Neither my preaching gift, my loved ones, nor friends were able to break me free from my internal prison. For days I the plaguing thoughts of chemotherapy and radiation grappled me, and eventually the fear of dying overtook me. No other time in my life was I more afraid than when I was nine years old and my mother got sick and I feared she would die.

As I said, the tests concluded I did not have prostate cancer which means I had spent precious moments of my life I will never be able to retrieve worrying about something that never happened. The stress I did to my heart worrying caused damage I will never be able to repair.

Such as the same with the story I opened this chapter with. While the tornado took Jonathan and Sandra by surprise, they survived it. How do you survive an unexpected storm? You ride them out. And as stated in the previous chapter, you trust God. I would bet that what makes unexpected storms so hard to deal with is the fact they catch you off guard and the fear of the unknown can often be worse than knowing the known. Ever gotten a phone call in the middle of the night that made you afraid to answer? Usually those calls are the ones everyone dreads because it typically means something terrible has happened. Up until you decide to answer the phone, each shrilling ring causes your heart to palpitate.

I'm reminded of the story found in the King James Version of Luke 8, verses 22 through 25.

"Now it came to pass on a certain day, that he went into a ship with his disciples: and he said unto them, 'Let us go over unto the other side of the lake.' And they launched forth. But as they sailed he fell asleep: and there came down a storm of wind on the lake; and they were filled with water, and were in jeopardy. And they came to him, and awoke him, saying, Master, master we perish. Then he arose, and rebuked the wind and the raging of the water: and they ceased, and there was a calm. And he said unto them, where is your faith? And they being afraid wondered, saying one to another, what manner of man is this! For he commandeth even the winds and water, and they obey him."

The King James Version of Mark 4 records it like this in verses 36 through 41:

"And when they had sent away the multitude, they took him even as he was in the ship. And there were also with him other little ships. And there arose a great storm of wind, and the waves beat into the ship, so that it was now full. And he was in the hinder part of the ship, asleep on a pillow: and they awake him, and say unto him, Master, carest thou not that we perish? And he arose, and rebuked the wind, and said unto the sea, 'Peace be still.' And the wind ceased, and there was a great calm. And he said unto them, 'Why are you so fearful? How is it that ye have no faith?' And they feared exceedingly, and said one to another, what manner of man is this, that even the wind and the sea obey him?"

Wow! That is what you call an unexpected storm!

Let's look at that text.

In both accounts, we see what was supposed to be a simple trip to the other side of the lake take a drastic turn for the worse, resulting in their boat nearly capsizing. As both Mark and Luke describe it, a storm of the wind, which was very likely what we know to be a hurricane, arose suddenly. How many of you know sometimes things happen so quickly you don't have time to pray, read your Bible, or call a prayer partner. All you have time to do is react. Most of us would have done the same thing the disciples did which was panic. Let's be honest, would you have thought to rebuke the wind? Even with the great level of faith I am sure you possess, when things catch you off guard you do not always do what you know you are supposed to do. The disciples were no different. They walked and talked with Jesus himself on a daily basis, but yet they were reprimanded by Jesus for having NO faith. Not for having a LITTLE faith, but, NO faith. Jesus suggests that his own disciples had no faith. Wow. The unexpectedness of the storm revealed their lack of faith. What does the storm reveal about you?

There is one interesting question in this text worth presenting. Why did they go to Jesus? Was it because they had seen Him perform miracles and they believed He could do something about the situation they were in? Well, let's say for all intent and purposes that is the case. Here then is the better question. Why were they astonished when He rebuked the wind causing the wind to obey if indeed they woke Him so he could do just that?

Here is what I believe. I think Jesus was upset because they lacked faith in His ability to calm the storm. I don't believe they were waking Him to perform a miracle, but I think they were waking him because they could not understand how He could be sleep when all hell was breaking loose around Him. Notice what they were concerned about when they got to the bottom of the ship. They asked Him if He cared. Not once did they beckon for the Master to exert His power to calm the raging sea. The real reason they went to Him was because they had a problem with Him resting in the midst of the storm.

Have you ever been going through so much that it seemed as if God did not care about what you were going through? Did it seem as if He was preoccupied with someone else's stuff so to the point that He'd forgotten about you? I know what it feels like to go through so much hell you begin to wonder if God is anywhere near. I know how it feels to be in the middle of trying to weather a storm without going to God about it every single day, every single hour, or every single minute. But, somehow you find yourself right back in His ear just in case He didn't hear you the first time.

I told you earlier in the chapter that the way to deal with an unexpected storm was to ride it out.

Here is the second way.

Relax.

Don't panic. Trust and take comfort in the fact that Jesus is on your boat. I am sure you have heard it preached before—when Jesus is on your boat, there is no way the waves of your storm can contain enough power to take you out. Have enough faith in Him to know that He at any given point in time can focus His attention on your circumstance, and declare peace.

Lastly, rest.

Yes, rest.

I know you are probably rolling your eyes at this because how insensitive of me is it to tell you to: 1) Ride it out; 2) Relax; 3) and Rest while you're going through.

I know how farfetched it may be to envision doing either of those when the devil seems to have his entire kingdom waging war against you. I know it seems crazy to encourage you to rest when you are in the heart of a storm. But, my brothers and sisters, you must learn how to rest. How do you rest? You don't rest IN your own abilities. But, you rest ON the promises of God. Rest assured that although the storm might have been unexpected, since you are in His will, He has no other choice but to take care of you. Remember, I told you it was Jesus' idea in the first place to take the trip to the other side of the lake. Since they were simply obeying Him by going, they should have known that He would make everything alright. The fact that Jesus would not put Himself in harm's way should have been enough for the disciples to believe they were going to make it out alive.

The next time you are blindsided by a storm you didn't expect to happen, I want you to first analyze if you are in the will of God and where He wants you to be. Because there is safety in the will of God. Nothing can harm you when you are where God wants you to be. That is why it is so important for a Christian to have a strong prayer life so you can stay in constant communication with God about His will, HIs desires, and His plan for your life.

Let me encourage you.

The plan of the enemy is to make you forget all God has brought you through in the past but in the time when life seems to be serving you total knockouts, do your best to reflect on the storms you have survived in the past. If God did it once can He not do it again? Of course He can. You are going to be just fine. You may have tears in your eyes as you are reading this. You may be on the verge of letting go. You may be close to throwing in the towel. But, I urge you and challenge you to remember that Jesus is in your boat and there is nothing going on that He is not in control of.

He's got you.

STORM SURVIVORS

William A. Jordan

Chapter Three

~

You're Not Under Attack-You're Tired

O n average, how many hours of sleep would you say you get per night? How often do you spend the weekends doing exactly what you want to do, going where you want to go, or having a meal that you enjoy without counting your caloric intake? When was the last time you took a family vacation or took a vacation day from work so you could take your kids to their favorite park or restaurant?

By now, I am sure you see a pattern in this book. I ask a lot of questions. They are asked because I want to provoke you to think. It is not all the time possible to change your circumstances but it is possible to make some changes that change you.

The questions above lead me to discuss a serious matter that has been a taboo subject in the church for too long. It is mental therapy. Do you know how many tongue talking, Bible toting Christians suffer silently with depression and suicidal thoughts? Many times they suffer because they refuse to get help. Especially in the African-American community, studies show that very few seek counseling or psychotherapy to assist them with dealing with the sickness of the mind. Often time Pastors do not want to discuss this or encourage our congregations to get help because we are not accustomed to preaching to people whose lives are whole and complete. But we are accustomed to preaching to folk dysfunction.

There are some storms you go through that are so devastating it is hard to immediately recover from them. You cannot all the time pray something away. Sometimes you need to talk to someone—vent. Sometimes you need to sit down and regroup. Sometime you need to cry until you feel better. Different storms require different recovery strategies. For example, when a person loses a loved one or goes through a divorce which has proven to have similar mental effects, there is nothing you can do but pray for their inner strength and give them time to heal.

A thunderstorm is the type of storm that will knock down trees or power lines at most, but hurricanes, tornados, and tsunamis are storms that can wipe out entire communities—even cities. So, if you are experiencing a thunderstorm in your life, you may be able to bounce back in a day or two—maybe even a week. But when a tornado-like storm rips through your life and shreds your heart to pieces, it may take months, even years, to recover. It kills me when we take for granted how something is affecting someone. Everything is not the devil. If I lose my mother, it is not the devil if you find me having a hard time dealing with her death. If I lose my spouse or one of my kids, it is not the devil if you find me crying myself to sleep at night or walking around with an unkempt beard. Again, I say, everything is not the devil. But, in the church, we have made everything so spiritual that we often fail to remember that we are spiritual beings operating in an earthly vessel. And this vessel comes with feelings and emotions that cause adverse or unusual reactions to hurt and pain.

As a Pastor I have had the opportunity to eulogize and bury quite a few people. Nothing angers me more than hearing someone telling the bereaved to not cry because their loved one is in a better place, is no longer suffering, or lived a long life. It infuriates me because it does not matter they are in a better place when the family want nothing more than to have them here with them on Earth. It matters not they are no longer suffering because just to hold their hand again, hear their voice again would be all they desired. It matters not if they lived to be eighty years old, or in some case, a hundred. The longer you have with a person the more attached you become to them. Overall my point is, we must give way to our super spiritual side at times and allow people to be what they are—human. If you are involved in a car crash that severs a body part, and you call me, I am going to pray for you after I call 911 or as I drive you to the hospital to get help. Now think about that for a second. Why do we rush people to the hospital to get medical attention for broken bones, slow beating hearts, renal failure, or any other disease or illness we feel is life threatening; yet, we try to pray away the illness of the mind? Something is wrong with that.

Depression is real. It is not all the time a spiritual attack. Sometimes you are depressed because you are tired and have overworked yourself to the point your body begins to react based on the strength of your mind, which is after all our central operating system. Healthy minds produce healthy bodies that produce healthy individuals. If your mind is not right, nothing about you will be right. A lot of you are mentally exhausted but instead of stopping to nurture yourself, you keep going, and eventually the exhaustion intensifies. Ultimately, this helps no one. Not you or anyone or anything you are affiliated with. Week after week, mentally exhausted people gather in their local churches expecting the Pastor to give them a Word from God that's going to give them the strength to go on, or as we say in church, press through. Sometimes I bet God wants to say, "Just go get some rest, my child."

Let me clarify what we are talking about as it relates to depression. Below is some information taken from ChristianityToday.com.

In order to distinguish severe or "major depression" from everyday blues, the American Psychiatric Association offers the following diagnostic criteria:

Major depression is diagnosed when an adult exhibits one or both of two core symptoms (depressed mood and lack of interest), along with four or more of the following symptoms, for at least two weeks: feelings of worthlessness or inappropriate guilt; diminished ability to concentrate or make decisions; fatigue; psychomotor agitation (cannot sit still) or retardation (just sitting around); insomnia or hypersomnia (sleeping too much); significant decrease or increase in weight or appetite; and recurrent thoughts of death or suicidal ideation.

This clinical definition is sterile, however, and fails to capture the unique quality of the severely depressed person's suffering.

Deep depression is *embodied emotional suffering*. It is not simply a state of mind or a negative view of life but something that affects our physical being as well. Signs of a severe episode of depression include unfounded negative evaluations of friends, family, and oneself, emotional "pain," physical problems such as lethargy, difficulty getting one's thoughts together, and virtually no interest in one's surroundings. Though most of us know at least an acquaintance who has committed suicide, this tragic act baffles us perhaps as much as it pains us. "I just don't understand," we say. The irony is that survivors of serious suicide attempts frequently reflect on those attempts with a similar attitude: "I have no idea what came over me." The pain and mental dysfunction of major depression are that deep.

However, we choose to define depression, both its frequency and its disruption of normal life are staggering. The World Health Organization named depression the second most common cause of disability worldwide after cardiovascular disease, and it is expected to become number one in the next ten years. In the United States, 5 to 10 percent of adults currently experience the symptoms of major depression (as previously defined), and up to 25 percent meet the diagnostic criteria during their lifetime, making it one of the most common conditions treated by primary care physicians. At any given time, around 15 percent of American adults are taking antidepressant medications.

Studies of religious groups, from Orthodox Jews to evangelical Christians, reveal no evidence that the frequency of depression varies across religious groups or between those who attend religious services and those who do not. So in a typical congregation of 200 adults, 50 attendees will experience depression at some point, and at least 30 are currently taking antidepressants.

How do we explain these numbers? In part, they result from a two-pronged shift in cultural attitudes about depression. Groups such as the National Alliance on Mental Illness and pharmaceutical companies have aggressively promoted the view that depression is not a character flaw but a biological problem (a disease) in need of a biological solution (a drug). The efforts to medicalize depression have helped to remove the stigma attached to it and convince the public that it's not something to hide. Consequently, depression has come out of the closet.

Some critics argue that along with the disease view of depression comes a lowered diagnostic threshold. Professors Allan Horwitz and Jerome Wakefield argue in *The Loss of Sadness* (Oxford, 2007) that psychiatrists no longer provide room for their clients' sadness or life's usual ups and downs, labeling even normal mood fluctuations "depression." (Everyday conversation reflects this assumption. When asked how we are doing, we commonly answer "great" or at least "good." If we reveal that we're "fine"—or worse, just "okay"—people tend to assume something is wrong and begin probing.)

Critics like Horwitz and Wakefield are half right. It is true that the mental health community has lowered the threshold for recognizing depression. Yet when we trace depression in the United States over the past 20 years using fixed criteria, we still see a significant increase in frequency. So although the numbers may be inflated, and this bump unquestionably serves the profit margins of pharmaceutical companies, we nevertheless have a substantial, documented increase to try to explain.

Our society has reaped considerable benefit from casting a wide net and assuming that everything caught is a disease. We now are more attuned to depression's burden of emotional suffering, better understand biological factors, and have medications that address those factors. We should be thankful for these significant gains.

No symptom is more central to depression than the loss of hope. The bible says in *Proverbs 13:12 says, "Hope deferred makes the heart sick: but when the desire cometh, it is a tree of life.*

The medical models come up short because they can only go as far as their understanding of the subject of the problem will take them. And both slight their subject: human beings. Cultural institutions and authorities may sometimes treat human beings as if we are nothing but brains in bodies, but this does not make it so. For those with eyes to see, the depression epidemic is in part a witness to the complexity of human nature. In particular, it reminds us that we are social and spiritual (as well as physical) creatures, and that a fallen society's afflictions are often inscribed on the bodies of its members. We have misjudged humanity if we expect our bodies to be impervious to social travail. *("And being in anguish, he prayed more earnestly, and his sweat was like drops of blood falling to the ground," Luke 22:44.)*

In fact, sometimes an episode of what looks like depression does not indicate that the human organism is malfunctioning, but is instead being true to her spiritual-social-physical nature. Embodied emotional pain can be an appropriate response to suffering in a world gone wrong. The author of Lamentations must have felt such pain as he gazed upon the destruction of Jerusalem. *"My eyes fail from weeping, I am in torment within, my heart is poured out on the ground because my people are destroyed, because children and infants faint in the streets of the city" Lamentations 2:11.*

Christians are called to weep with those who weep, and should welcome emotional pain that results from empathy and draws us alongside the afflicted. If we have grown numb to the pain and suffering around us, we have lost our humanity.

Herein lies the point to all of this and I cannot stress this enough: Get. Some. Help. I don't care if people attack your spiritual foundation for going to sit on somebody's couch. You go and sit on that couch and tell a stranger all of your business if you must do so. Whatever you do, please do not allow depression to mature and take over your life.

Speaking of, that leads me to discuss suicide—a rare topic mentioned in the church. However, do you know that there are several people walking around you and sitting next to you in church that's on the verge of giving up? There are more praise and worship leaders and minstrels than you probably know who get up in church on Sunday's and do their best singing unto the Lord; Pastors and ministers who get up and preach expository sermons; but, as soon as the microphone is off and the crowd has cleared, they go home to wrestle with thoughts of taking their life.

Dr. Charles Spurgeon, one of the world's greatest known theologians, suffered with depression and suicidal thoughts. He was one who spent hours upon hours studying the Word of God, which proves to me that you can be deeply rooted in the word and the word deeply rooted in you, and still be depressed.

What would you do if one of the times you asked someone how they were doing and they responded by saying they were about to end their life? Have we gotten so accustomed to hearing the normal run of the mill jargon with people responding that they are blessed and highly favored of God and empowered to prosper? One thing that gets the blood boiling in my veins is when I ask someone how they are doing and they basically respond with their daily confession opposed to just saying how they are doing. If someone asks you how you are doing, there is no need to quote a ton of scriptures. Either you are doing okay or you are not. It really is that simple. If you are not doing okay and if you are talking to someone you trust with the intimate details of what is going on, then talk to them openly. Holding problems in and internally absorbing your pain in an effort to vie for the Christian of the Year award, is asinine, and can prove to be detrimental. Most of the people who choose to not get help of any sort, usually end up committing suicide, and as we see so prevalently in our society, they take the lives of others as well.

When you read the book of Psalms and see the writings of David, you will discover a man—a King—who was very transparent about what he was going through. You would think David suffered with bipolar disorder, because in one chapter alone he will go from crying out to God about his troubles and inability to go any further, to praising God and bringing to remembrance the battles he had won with God's help.

There are seven suicides recorded in the Bible. They were:

1) Abimelech, who lacked personal identity. (Judges 9:52-54)
2) Samson died for a cause he believed in and for revenge. (Judges 16:25-30)
3) Saul was stressed out, unable to live up to certain expectations, felt rejected and a failure. (I Samuel 31:4)
4) Saul's Armor Bearer, wanted to die with his employer. It was an impulse decision (I Samuel 31:5),
5) Ahithophel was bitter because his advice wasn't followed. Basically, he didn't get his way. (I Kings 17:23)
6) Zimri had an issue with authority. (I Kings 16:15-20)
7) Judas was depressed and consumed by guilt. (Matthew 27:3-5)

Here are a couple of things I want to leave you with.

God has a great and wonderful plan for your life. God has created us in His image and with a purpose. Not only that, regardless to what is going on, there is a divine plan for your life as well.

"For I know the plans I have for you, declares the Lord, plans to prosper you and not to harm you, plans to give you hope and a future. (Jeremiah 29:11)

Finally, Jesus wants you to have life and life more abundantly.

"The thief comes only to steal and kill and destroy; I have come that they may have life, and have it to the full. (John 10:10)

Beloved, here is your challenge. Before you are quick to think you are under spiritual attack, assess your life and see what lifestyle changes can be made to make it easier on you. If you are working a job that brings you no peace, then leave. If you are in an unhealthy relationship that is bringing you more stress than it is peace, then leave. If you are in over your head with bills, then downsize.

Nothing is worth your life and the last thing you want is to survive the storm but not survive YOU.

Be happy.

Just live your life.

STORM SURVIVORS

Chapter Four

~

Lord, Help Me Survive the Storm I Created

In the previous chapter I indirectly mentioned that some things we go through are brought upon by us. The devil didn't do it. He didn't make you do it. You just did it. On your own.

As much as I hate the devil, I can honestly say he has often been erroneously blamed for our bad decisions. For example, if you have hypertension and your physician advises you to not eat pork, chocolate, or anything that may send your blood pressure through the roof, but you decide to do it anyway, whose fault is that? How silly does it look to rebuke your swollen feet and high blood pressure instead of just eating right? What you should have been doing was turning down those golden fried pork chops and crispy bacon. Now that may register in your mind as a silly example but if you be honest with yourself you know it is the truth. Sometimes we make dumb moves and instead of accepting it and owning it when it's time to face the consequences; we blame the devil or make excuses.

When this book is released, the Christmas holiday season will have just passed and I can't help but wonder how many shoppers emptied—or near emptied—their bank accounts to purchase gifts they really could not afford to give.

Every year I see several people with a *generic* budget but *Gucci* shopping in an effort to impress people who will go back to living their comfortable lives while the person doing the big spending is left to pay credit card and department store debt.

Debt is one of the top three leading causes of stress, and is listed as one of the top five reasons many marriages end in divorce. Lest I detour from my message of survival and jump into a lesson on finances, I'll just throw in for good measure that not all debt is bad debt. I am speaking more so about the debt you don't have to get in. Debt you create because you are trying to maintain a façade or mimic the life of another. I said something similar to this in the beginning of the book, but why is everybody trying to keep up with the Jones'. First of all, who are the Jones'? Let's say they really exist. Whoever they are, no one knows if they are really even paying their bills. No one knows if they are happy with all of the things they have. No one knows if they are doing all they can to maintain their peace. The point: Do you and stop worrying about what someone else is doing. More people are going to their graves worried about what everyone else is doing instead of being concerned with them own selves.

We are living in a world where social media has pretty much become the medium for keeping in touch with friends—and some family—as well as for keeping tabs on other people's lives. Individuals will get on social media and tweet or post everything from how they are feeling, what they ate for breakfast, or the new home they just closed on. It enables us to have a sneak peek into the lives of other people. While I strongly encourage people to stay abreast update to date with new forms of communication such as Twitter, Facebook, Instagram, Socialcam, and others; it saddens me when I see people trying to develop an identity on one of these platforms. Listen, you are uniquely made. You are not defined by the number of followers you have on Twitter or the number of friends you have on Facebook. The summation of who you are is not totaled based on the amount of retweets you got or likes to your status. As I myself browse my own Timeline and Newsfeed, I run across people aiming to get the approval, or gain the acceptance, of people they do not know. It cripples my heart because I remember times in my life where my own self-esteem was so low, I felt I had to *do* something to be accepted versus *be* somebody.

You may be wondering what any of the above have to do with anything storm related. I'm glad you're interested in knowing. I will tell you how. A lot of the storms we are in are self-induced by wrong decisions and choices. Keeping up with someone else and patterning your life after them is not only absurd, but can be dangerous especially when things may not go as well for you as it has for someone else. For example, one man may be able to commit adultery and never get caught. Another man may see that, gain the courage to do it, yet end up getting caught and exposed. Can the man who got caught blame anyone but himself? Can he rebuke the devil that is he feels is in his wife who now wants to leave because the marriage covenant has been broken? Absolutely not. He must own up to the part he played in the matter. What about a single mother who spends all of her money on designer clothes, purses, and shoes but is always broke when it is time to pay the rent or mortgage? How silly does she appear rebuking the demon that's stealing her finances? Very silly. There is no need to rebuke a demon for simply taking what you handed over to him. Think about that. How much are you handing over to the enemy versus what he is actually taking from you?

A great Biblical example of a negative result of a bad decision is David and Bathsheba committing adultery and a child is conceived. But, read what happens. This passage is taken from *II Samuel 12:12-24. (MSG)*

"Then David confessed to Nathan, "I've sinned against God." Nathan pronounced, "Yes, but that's not the last word. God forgives your sin. You won't die for it. But because of your blasphemous behavior, the son born to you will die. After Nathan went home, God afflicted the child that Uriah's wife bore to David, and he came down sick. David prayed desperately to God for the little boy. He fasted, wouldn't go out, and slept on the floor. The elders in his family came in and tried to get him off the floor, but he wouldn't budge. Nor could they get him to eat anything. On the seventh day the child died. David's servants were afraid to tell him. They said, "What do we do now? While the child was living he wouldn't listen to a word we said. Now, with the child dead, if we speak to him there's no telling what he'll do." David noticed that the servants were whispering behind his back, and realized that the boy must have died. He asked the servants, "Is the boy dead?" "Yes," they answered."He's dead." David got up from the floor, washed his face and combed his hair, put on a fresh change of clothes, then went into the sanctuary and worshipped. Then he came home and asked for a something to eat. They set it before him and he ate. His servants asked him, "What's going on with you? While the child was alive you fasted and wept and stayed up all night. Now that he's dead, you get up and eat." "While the child was alive," he said, "I fasted and wept, thinking God might have mercy on me and the child would live. But now that he's dead, why fast? Can I bring him back now? I can go to him, but he can't come to me."

What a heartbreaking story that is. As a father myself, I

cannot imagine what was going through David's mind as he prepared to go and view his son's body and make the preparations that would lead the boy to his final resting place. The biggest question that looms in my mind is: How did David live with knowing that his sin—a terrible decision—was the cause of his son's death? It must have been hard to face the reflection in the mirror for a long time after his son's death knowing that it was his fault. Although the Lord had already sent the prophet to warn him and to let him know that his own personal life would be saved, I am almost willing to bet that David would have much preferred his life be taken and his child's life be spared. No parent wants to bury their child. No parent wants to hold the lifeless hand of a child and whisper goodbyes. I can almost guarantee that the level of regret he felt was unprecedented, and if by any chance he could have turned back the hands of mother time, he would have done so, and made a better choice.

I am not trying to scare you with the above text because not all the time do bad decisions result in the death of someone you love. I am asking you to take inventory of your life and look at the things you are blaming on the devil, or are mad with God about, and see if by any chance if what is happening is your fault.

However it goes, God is a faithful and just God, willing to forgive us of our sins. It does not matter what you have done or how low you have sank, His grace is sufficient for you. Contrary to what you may think, God is not mad at you. When you ask for forgiveness, it is automatically granted. Don't walk around harboring guilt about yesterday's bad decisions, but embrace that your loving and merciful God continues to give you chance after chance to get it right.

If I were honest with myself, it was in the storms I created, that I learned the most valuable lessons. I know we live in a time where most don't believe in chastising children via spankings, or what I know as, whippings. Children get sent to rooms now without the privilege of using such luxuries as: Playstations, Wii, iPads, and cell phones. When I was growing up, we did not have any of those things. We were blessed to have any form of entertainment outside of the rocks, sticks, and grasshoppers we caught in the backyard. But, I grew up in a home where spankings were given as needed. Before my mom would light into my behind, she would always ask, "Didn't I tell you not to do that?" I would in turn shake my head in agreement. Then the following question would be, "Well, why did you do it?" My answer: a shrug of the shoulders. Who knows why anybody does wrong when you know you know the right thing to do. But, my mother needed to make sure I understood why I was about to get a beating. Looking back on it, while it did not feel good to have a belt attacking my backside, I can appreciate that discipline now that I am older. Here is what I know. If you keep getting a beating about the same thing, over and over, eventually you get tired of feeling pain, learn the lesson, and decide to make better choices.

I guarantee if you keep going through a financial storm due to overspending and a lack of budgeting, I can almost assure you the next time you get a bonus, raise, or increase, you will think twice before going out to splurge and loosely spend money. Without a doubt, if you grow weary of being sick all of the time due to a spirit of gluttony, you will eventually push the plate back. If you get fed up with being in an unproductive, non-loving relationship, you will release that person faster than a New York minute.

Bottom line, when you get tired of being sick and tired, you will do whatever is necessary to chase and capture your peace. You will do what is necessary to track down and hold on to your happiness. You will do whatever is necessary to find and secure your joy.

Sometimes it takes falling into the traps our actions set, for us to really get it.

In case you have discovered that some of the storms you are in right now are ones that were self-induced, I want to close out this chapter by praying with you a very simple prayer.

Dear Lord,

I know I don't have to tell you this because you already know. But, I have made some decisions that have landed me in a prison of guilt and I need you to help me get free. Lord, I am asking that you forgive me for the wrong things I have done, wash me in your blood, and give e a new start and a new opportunity to get things right in my life. My heart's desire is to do what is pleasing in your sight and I am asking you today to help me do that. My intentions are often good, but every time I try to do good, evil is always present. I am asking you to allow the Holy Spirit to keep me even in the times I don't want to be kept so that going forward I can bypass the pain I bring upon myself due to disobedience. Thank you, Lord, for all that you have done, all that you are doing, and all that you are going to do.

This is my prayer in Jesus' name.

Amen.

William A. Jordan

Chapter Five

~

Bend But Don't Break

E ven after storms end there are some that leave scars that serve as reminders of the permanent damage left behind.

Imagine the current lives of the parents of the many teenagers who have been gunned downed on the cold, violent streets of Chicago; or the divorce that took place between a couple who had been married for twenty years; or the family who lost their home to foreclosure and are struggling to find shelter for their children; or the child who lost both their parents in a car accident and are forced to live from one foster care home to another; or the elderly man or woman whose body is stricken with cancer.

When those type things happen, you never forget them. You may learn to live through them, but they change you forever. I am certain if you look on your body there are scars that are still there that remind you of a fall you took as a child. While the pain is no longer felt, the scar is there— forever. Even when bones are broken, they may heal, but it is not uncommon to feel an ache or pain ten years later, when it gets cold or rains outside.

But have you ever gone through something so bad you

wish the healing process would hurry up and take its course? Have you ever experienced so much pain you thought your heart would literally stop beating?

One of my best friends in the world has brain cancer. On at least two occasions she has been given a death sentence, but has lived through them both, and continues to defy the odds and astound the physicians who are yet to figure out how she is still alive with such an advanced stage of cancer. But, I vividly remember talking to her one day when her body was in excruciating pain. It pained my heart to hear the agony in her voice and it pained me even more to hear her tell me she was giving up. She had decided she could no longer live through the pain and pleaded for me to understand that she wanted to die. Now the preacher in me stood up and began to declare life over her. I began to quote all of the scriptures that we use when we are facing turbulent winds. As her Pastor, I prayed, and as her friend, I fussed at her for even having the notion that she would give up.

In hindsight, I can empathize with her. I have no clue how it feels to have a germ zipping through my body, slowly eating away at my insides. But I do know how it feels to want to give up. To want to wave goodbye to this world because life has grown too heavy for me to bear. I said this before, but even the strongest faith is tested. There have been many days in my Pastoral tenure I wanted to throw up the deuces, walk away from my calling, and possibly go back to being a broke surgical technician at the hospital I worked at for many years. There have been days so bad that not even a meal from my favorite restaurant, Capital Grille, aided in my internal relief. Yet, I put on my classic, black suits week after week, chalked it up and pressed on.

Tell me, what do you do when you are at a breaking point? When life's winds are blowing so strong you are tossed on every side. When it appears the violent wind is snuffing out the very breath in your body.

One of my favorite passages of scripture to read during times like that is found in *II Corinthians 4:8-9 (KJV)*.

"We are troubled on every side, yet not distressed; we are perplexed, but no in despair; persecuted, but not forsaken; cast down, but not destroyed."

It picks up in verse 16 saying, *"For which cause we faint not; but though our outward man perish, yet the inward man is renewed day by day. For our light affliction, which is but for a moment, worketh for us a far more exceeding eight of glory; while we look not at the things which are seen, but at the things which are not seen: for the things which are seen are temporal; but the things which are not seen are eternal.*

The enemy wants you to break because he knows how hard it is for brokenness to heal. Beloved, what I am saying to you is some storms come specifically to break you. The devil is not concerned with you just getting an injury and having to sit out of *a* game, he is aiming to break you enough to put you out of *the* game. His goal is to get you so broken and discouraged until you have no strength to persevere. You've read and heard that the race is not given to the swift or the strong, but to the one who endures to the end. He is not after your start; he is after your finish.

Some of the worst breaking points come after some of your best victories. Ever have a season where it seems everything was going the way you wanted it to go and no sooner than you can get comfortable, mess hits the fan?

Imagine getting a job promotion on Friday and then walk into your office on Monday and all of a sudden the entire staff has decided to become your newfound enemies, consequently making your job difficult to do or tolerate. Imagine a couple celebrating their wedding anniversary on Saturday and then on Monday morning instead of having breakfast together, they are in their attorney's office filing for divorce. How can that be?

Look below at the text found in *I Kings 19:1-7 (KJV)*.

And Ahab told Jezebel all that Elijah had done, and withal how he had slain all the prophets with the sword. Then Jezebel sent a messenger unto Elijah, saying, So let the gods do to me, and more also, if I make not thy life as the life of one of them by to morrow about this time. And when he saw that, he arose, and went for his life, and came to Beersheba, which belongeth to Judah, and left his servant there. But he himself went a day's journey into the wilderness, and came and sat down under a juniper tree: and he requested for himself that he might die; and said, It is enough; now, O LORD, take away my life; for I am not better than my fathers. And as he lay and slept under a juniper tree, behold, then an angel touched him, and said unto him, Arise and eat. And he looked, and, behold, there was a cake baken on the coals, and a cruse of water at his head. And he did eat and drink, and laid him down again. And the angel of the LORD came again the second time, and touched him, and said, Arise and eat; because the journey is too great for thee.

If you go back a chapter, you will read how Elijah called fire down from Heaven and it led to the destruction of the prophets of Baal. I don't know how you feel about it, but if the Lord had just shown Himself to me in such a demonstrative way, I would have been on a spiritual high. Yet, Elijah found himself running from his life. Particles of fear and hopelessness slowly infiltrated his mind and spirit, and he found himself exemplifying the classic signs of depression. He isolated himself by leaving his passé, he took cover under a juniper tree and went to sleep to try and escape reality, and he lost his appetite.

I must interject this to combat the notion that I would have been on a spiritual high if the Lord had shown up for me in the way He showed up for Elijah. I feel a pang of conviction. God just said to me, "How many times have I answered your prayers yet when something new comes up, you doubt me as if I never did a single thing?" Have many times do we testify that God gave us the money to pay our bills, He healed our bodies, He saved our children, He made a way out of no way; but as soon as trouble arise again, we get spiritual amnesia.

Elijah had just seen what God could do. His relationship and connection with the Lord was proven that day when fire fell from Heaven. But, how many of you know the enemy will turn up the heat just after you have had an encounter with God? In this case, Jezebel had no power. But sometimes a threat will mask as the truth. That is why it is so important to do all you can to protect your thoughts. Spiritual warfare will never cease. The devil will always be after you. And when you are between breaking and breakthrough, hold on to what you know to be true about God. You know if He brought you out once, He can do it again.

The angels visited Elijah once he had mentally given up. They did not come with a deep word. They didn't come with a vial of anointing oil and start slathering it all over his body. They did not lay a single hand on him. They simply brought him some food. It goes back to my earlier point. There are times when practicality is needed and not spirituality. They allowed him to rest after he ate. Basically they allowed him to bend, but stayed around to make sure he had the nutrients he needed to not break. Food energizes your mind and since the war was in Elijah's mind that is what they focused on. Because nothing had actually happened. A simple threat caused him to react the way he did. And you know how it is when you *think* something is going to happen. Elijah had probably already envisioned his funeral services. He probably saw in his mind his own beheading. And again, all because of a threat!

But if you keep reading that text on down to verse ten, the Word of the Lord comes. After Elijah's body had been nourished, it was time for his spirit man to be ministered to. And, my friends, if you are going to survive life's storms, if you are going to bend and not break, it is imperative for you to allow the Word of God to give life to your spirit. You cannot make it without a Word from the Lord. One word from the Lord can change your very life. It changed Elijah's. Elijah's spirit man stood back up and he got back on the battlefield for the Lord.

The devil's threat drove him away from his ministry, but the Lord's calling on his life pushed him back into it.

The devil's threat caused him to be depressed, but the prophetic assignment recharged him.

The devils' threat sent him into the wilderness, but the Lord's voice got him out.

When he left the desert nothing had changed in his circumstances. He just had a Word. A word will give you strength you never knew you had. A word will lead you to your peace, prosperity, and promise.

So you can serve notice to those who thought it was over for you that you are yet alive. The storm might have caused you to bend but you didn't break. It didn't take you out as it might have been predicted to. In Elijah's case, Jezebel was no match for his Jehovah!

We all know the story of Job. Job was sitting at home one day minding his own business when in a matter of minutes he had lost it all. Children, property, investments...gone. Now, I thought about putting this story in the chapter about unexpected storms, but I saved it for this chapter because Job is a prime example of one who weathers a storm that bends him but not break him. Many days he cried, he pouted, he cried out to God wondering what he had done to bring such calamity on his life. His own wife told him to curse God and die. While he did not maintain his demeanor, he maintained his declaration. He says in ***Job 13:15- "Thou he slay me, yet will I trust Him: but I will maintain my own ways before Him."*** That blessed me right there! Job declares that it does not matter how rough it gets. No matter how the storm was raging in his life, his soul was anchored in the Lord. He declares that even though he lost his property, he did not lose his position in his faith. Can you say that today? Can you stand when the bottom is falling out from underneath your feet? Can you remain encouraged through disappointing situations?

We all know how Job's story ends. God gave him more in the end that what he began with. What blessings are we possibly missing out on because we allow the storm to break us? Strong trees can endure the worst of storms. The wind may cause them to lift their branches and wave to the oncoming force, but they hold on. Beloved, hold on, because your change *is* going to come!

William A. Jordan

Chapter Six

~

God Has Not Forgotten About You

Ten-year old Whitney watched the clock intently as the minutes and the seconds ticked by. It was nearing time for the bell to ring, signaling not only the end of class, but the beginning of Pancake Day. Whitney loved Pancake Day because pancakes were one of her favorite foods and also because it was the day they allowed the parents to come and have breakfast with their kids. Whitney's dad who was a very busy businessman, and whom she rarely saw, always made time to attend this special day knowing it was so important to her.

Finally the bell rang, and an excited Whitney sprang from her desk, rushed to her locker, put her books away, and practically sprinted to the next classroom where they were only going to assemble for the purpose of lining up to go to the cafeteria. Whitney quickly took her place in line and stood with baited breath as she waited for Ms. Homer, her teacher, to announce they were ready to go. After what seemed like an eternity, the children were walking in a single file line headed to meet their parents. The doors to the lunchroom swung open and children with glee on their face beamed as they each found their parents.

Whitney's smile began to fade and her heart began to race as she scanned the cafeteria. There was no sight of her dad. She walked around the room hoping that somehow she had overlooked him. She watched as the other kids sat down with their pancakes and parents, and with her stomach feeling as it was twisting in knots, she made her way to her teacher who was standing with the kids whose parents did not show up. Fighting her tears and willing herself not to cry, she accepted that her father would not show up. She was sure he remembered, as he had called the night before to confirm. She made excuses for him in her mind and concluded there had to be a perfectly good reason he would miss such an important day to her.

Ms. Homer ushered the remaining kids to the food line where they each took a tray of pancakes and went to the table designated for the students with no guests. As Whitney sat the tray on the table, the tears she had fought so hard to keep from falling fell anyway. They fell rapidly. Before she knew it her shoulders were slumped over and her head hung in disappointment. Her father had not shown up. He wasn't coming.

Lost in dismay, Whitney felt a hand touch her shoulder. She didn't even bother to look up because she was certain it was just Ms. Homer consoling her, and she did not want to see the stares of the other kids and their parents as she cried a river. But then she heard his voice. The voice of her father.

"Whitney, why are you crying, my child? I'm a little late but I'm here."

"Daddy," she exclaimed. "I thought you had forgotten about me."

"You are my daughter and I will never forget about you. I love you. Now, let's enjoy these pancakes."

Can you recall any moments like that in your life? Moments when you thought God had forgotten about you? Moments where you thought He would not show up when you needed Him the most? Moments where you felt like your Heavenly Father had set you up by promising to come through for you but in actuality wouldn't?

I can't speak for anyone else other than myself, but, I've had plenty of days when I felt that way. I don't think I've ever really questioned my Father's love *for* me but I have questioned his devotion *to* me. It must have hurt the father in the above story to see his child crying because she didn't think he would come. Imagine how our Father feels when we cry for the same reason. As a parent it would disturb me if I walked into my house and my son and daughter were sitting around crying and stressing out over whether they would have food for dinner. As their father, it is my job to make sure their needs are provided. It is my job to make sure they have some of the desires of their heart. It would be outright insulting to me if they took over my responsibilities simply because they believed I was unable to handle them myself.

I think we should give God more credit than we do. Have you ever stopped to think about the fact He has been ruling the world since day one? He is God. He is the manufacturer of our very existence but He is often not trusted to completely operate our lives. We will tell him to take the wheel but the moment He makes a turn we don't like or didn't foresee, we snatch the wheel back and place Him in the passenger seat. In essence, via our actions, we say to God, "I don't trust that you know what you are doing so I am taking over myself." I can only imagine what the Lord must think of his wayward, partially insane children at times.

The Bible is full of instances where individuals believed God had forgotten about them. One of the most classic ones is the story of Abraham and Sarah. We know how the story goes. They were well into age before their promised child that had been promised many years prior to his actual coming, showed up on the scene. They were so sure God had forgotten about them they took it upon themselves to go and create their own quick fix. It's no secret they solicited the participation of Hagar and she bore a son, Ishmael, for Abraham. We know the problems this created because God had NOT forgotten about them and in the appointed time, Isaac, the promised child, was born. Not only did they live to see their promised child, but what blesses me is they lived to see him grow up. What a faithful God He is.

Another Biblical account that comes to mind and fits this narrative perfectly is found in **Exodus 16:2-35 (Amplified).** Take a moment to read the following story and as you read pay close attention to the complaints of the children of Israel and God's response to them.

And the whole congregation of Israel murmured against Moses and Aaron in the wilderness, and said to them, Would that we had died by the hand of the Lord in the land of Egypt, when we sat by the fleshpots and ate bread to the full; for you have brought us out into this wilderness to kill this whole assembly with hunger. Then the Lord said to Moses, Behold, I will rain bread from the heavens for you; and the people shall go out and gather a day's portion every day, that I may prove them, whether they will walk in My law or not. On the sixth day they shall prepare to bring in twice as much as they gather daily. So Moses and Aaron said to all Israel, at evening you shall know that the Lord has brought you out from the land of

*Egypt, and in the morning you shall see the glory of the Lord, for He hears your murmurings against the Lord. For what are we, that you murmur against us? And Moses said, [This will happen] when the Lord gives you in the evening flesh to eat and in the morning bread to the full, because the Lord has heard your grumblings which you murmur against Him; what are we? Your murmurings are not against us, but **against the** Lord. And Moses said to Aaron, Say to all the congregation of Israel, Come near before the Lord, for He has heard your murmurings. And as Aaron spoke to the whole congregation of Israel, they looked toward the wilderness, and behold, the glory of the Lord appeared in the cloud! The Lord said to Moses, I have heard the murmurings of the Israelites; speak to them, saying, At twilight you shall eat meat, and between the two evenings you shall be filled with bread; and you shall know that I am the Lord your God. In the evening quails came up and covered the camp; and in the morning the dew lay round about the camp. And when the dew had gone, behold, upon the face of the wilderness there lay a fine, round and flake like thing, as fine as hoarfrost on the ground. When the Israelites saw it, they said one to another, Manna [What is it?]. For they did not know what it was. And Moses said to them, this is the bread which the Lord has given you to eat. This is what the Lord has commanded: Let every man gather of it as much as he will need, an omer for each person, according to the number of your persons; take it, every man for those in his tent. The [people] did so, and gathered some more, some less. When they measured it with an omer, he who gathered much had nothing over, and he who gathered little had no lack; each gathered according to his need. Moses said; Let none of it be left until morning. But they did not listen to Moses; some of them left of it until morning, and it bred worms, became foul, and stank; and Moses was angry with them. They gathered it every morning, each as much as he needed, for when the sun became hot it melted. And on the sixth day they gathered twice as much bread, two omers for each person; and all the leaders of the congregation came and told Moses. He said to them, The Lord has said, Tomorrow is a solemn rest, a holy Sabbath to* *the Lord; bake and boil what you will bake and boil today; and all that remains over put aside for you to keep until morning. They laid it aside till morning, as Moses told them; and it did not become foul, neither was it wormy. Moses said, Eat that today, for today is a Sabbath to the Lord. Today you shall find none in the field. Six days you shall gather it, but on the seventh day, the Sabbath, there shall be none. On the seventh day some of the people went out to gather, but they found none. The Lord said to Moses, How long do you [people] refuse to keep my commandments and my laws? See, the Lord has given you the Sabbath; therefore He gives you on the sixth day the bread for two days; let every man remain in his place; let no man leave his place on the seventh day. So the people rested on the seventh day. The house of Israel called the bread manna; it was like coriander seed, white, and it tasted like wafers made with honey. Moses said, this is what the Lord commands, Take an omer of it to be kept throughout your generations, that they may see the bread with which I fed you in the wilderness when I brought you out of the land of Egypt. And Moses said to Aaron, Take a pot and put an omer of manna in it, and lay it up before the Lord, to be kept throughout your generations. As the Lord commanded Moses, Aaron laid it up before the Testimony to be kept [in the ark]. And the Israelites ate manna forty years, until they came to a habitable land; they ate the manna until they came to the border of the land of Canaan.*

The children of Israel really thought the Lord would deliver them from out of Egypt just to get them to the wilderness and let them die. Brothers and sisters, do you really think the Lord would allow you to survive the last storm to let this storm kill you? Of course not. Look closely at the text. He knew exactly what they needed before they needed it. He knew His children had to be fed, so to make sure they were taken care of, God installed a kitchen in Heaven. And out of Heaven's stove came pieces of sweet bread. He didn't just give them food, He gave them good food! The Word tells us that no good thing will he withhold from us. Now if God can have Heaven cook up some sweet rolls, and pour them straight from the baker's basket, what more can He and will He do for us? Is He not the same God yesterday, today, and forever more?

Furthermore, God is not slack concerning His promises and that thing (s) He promised you, no matter how long ago it was, is STILL coming to pass. By now you know I like to refer back to sayings from the old saints of Zion, and here is a perfect place to include one. Old church mothers would say, "He may not come when you want Him, but He is always on time." You may think He's not going to show up, but you can believe that God does grand finales well. I don't care if it's the last second on the clock, if there is a second, that's enough time for Him to do a work. He's God and He don't need any help. Not from you or from me. He's been carrying the entire world in His hands since before you were ever thought about and He's never slipped and dropped it.

Children of God, If He can take care of your great-grandmother, grandmother, and your mother down through the years, I promise He is going to take care of you.

You don't have to worry or fret, God has not forgotten about you.

Chapter Seven

~

You're Almost There-Don't Give Up

The devil's goal is to get you to give up just before you cross the finish line. One of his best tactics of doing this is to keep moving the finish line so you fail to see that you're making progress. This is meant to tire you out because he knows that if you ever get the resilience you need to persevere, you will be a force to reckon with. There are a lot of people who could do great damage to the kingdom of darkness, but we will never know who they are for many of them have taken a seat on the sidelines of life. Can you imagine watching a football or basketball game and all of the star players were on the bench? Of course not. I wish I could sit from the seat of God and look at the many Christians across the world who are operating lower than their potential because they've grown weary. I bet there are a massive number of people who were once on fire for God but the storms of life weighed them down so to the point they lost their fire, passion, and zeal.

Child of God, can I encourage you? *Galatians 6:9 says, "And let us not be weary in well doing: for in due season we shall reap, if we faint not."* The first thing I want you to know is you are doing well. I know things have been hard. I know the road has been tough, but considering all of you've been through, you have done well. The fact that you are still in your mind and not sitting in the corner of a room the size of a prison cell waiting for medication is a testament of just how well you've done. The fact that you were able to forgive those who hurt you and pray for them in the midst of them doing you wrong is a testament that you've done well. The fact that you find a way to get out of your bed, go to work, care for your family, and still serve the Lord, is a testament that you've done well. Some of you know you were supposed to have lost it by now, but the Lord has kept you in perfect peace. No, you may not have made all of the right decisions. You may not have stayed on course, but you kept going, and that is enough for me to say, you've done well.

A lot of us give up right before we enter our *due* season. The Bible clearly tells us that the only way to get what's due to us is to hang on and faint not. How many times do we forfeit our blessings because we give up? How many blessings go unclaimed because we throw in the towel?

Here's what I want you to do. I want you to tap into your spirit and ask God to give you a revival in your spirit. I want you to get into your prayer closet and seek God like never before. The Kingdom of God needs you. I believe there is a prayer warrior inside of you. I believe there is a prophetic word in you that need to come out. I believe that there is a song in your spirit that needs to be heard. Will the real you please stand up?

You are victorious.

You are more than a conqueror.

As a matter of fact, you need to confess that on a daily basis. Do not allow the enemy to tell you who you are. Do not allow him to suppress and stifle you another day. You are closer to the end of your storm than you realize. Get up, wash your face, and press you way.

Ladies, it's time you let go of the hurt of the past. Do something for yourself. Go and get your hair done again. If you can't grow it, weave it. Get you some make-up, put on your heels, and strut with the confidence that you are a winner. More importantly, you are the epitome of an over comer. That storm really did come to take you out, but, my God, you are still here. You survived!

Fellas, stop feeling like a failure. Things may not have turned out like you wanted it to. You may not be financially where you thought you would be by now, but it really is alright. You still have time. Take what you have and make it work. Stop walking around with your head held down. You have no reason at all to be ashamed any longer. Your past does not dictate your future. What you did in the days of your youth has long ago been forgotten by the Lord. He has given you another opportunity, and I ask you, what will you do with it? Put your suit on, get a fresh cut, and go back out there and be the King you were created to be. Our families are counting on us, brother, to be the heads of our homes. They are counting on us to be strong, powerful leaders. God left us with the dominion and it is past time that we take our rightful place.

The only failure in life is failing to try again.

I pray this chapter will reignite something within you, my brother and my sister, to get up and give life a try one more time. I believe there is a little something left in you that desire to be excellent and great, but you are afraid. Afraid of disappointment. Afraid to be hurt again. Afraid that it may not work. But, within you is the power of resurrection.

You can get up.

You can start over.

You can try again.

The woman with the issue of blood suffered through this for twelve years. The Bible says she spent all of her money going from one doctor to the next, so to the point it practically bankrupts her. But, even after twelve years, no health insurance, enduring castigation from the community; when Jesus comes through her town holding a crusade, she finds the strength to get up, get dressed, and make her way to him. She had no idea if He could help her or if she would even get to Him, but she tried anyway. She left home not knowing what she would encounter. She left home not knowing if she would be stopped.

As she made her way, she had to press through the other people who were falling at his feet.

She had to make her way past the people who were surrounding Him seeking their own miracles. She did not care where He was on His way to; she just knew that she was in need of a miracle. And her need for a miracle was greater than any desire she may have had to stay in her place of desperation. I am sure the voices in her head mocked her as she got dressed. Mocked her as she walked out of the door and saw the swarm of people trying to get his attention. But, in spite of it all, we all know she got her healing after having touched the hem of the master's garment.

How desperate are you to make it to the Master? How driven are you to get what God has promised you? How determined are you to keep going to see what the end is going to bring?

I cannot promise you will not face anymore trials.

I wish I could tell you that you've jumped your last hurdle. But, I cannot.

I cannot promise you've cried your last tear.

But, here is what I can tell you.

I can tell you your latter will be greater than your former.

I can tell you your best days are ahead of you.

I can tell you God is going to restore to you what the enemy thought he got away with.

So, hold on, dear soldier. Don't you dare give up, don't you dare give in. You have come too far to give up now!

William A. Jordan

Chapter Eight

~

You WILL Survive

I know you saw it, but look at the title of this chapter again.

Now, say it aloud.

Say it over and over until it gets into your spirit.

Why do I want you to do that? Because according to the Word of God, you have an assurance that you will be fine.

Jeremiah 29:11 (KJV) says, "For I know the thoughts that I think toward you, saith the LORD, thoughts of peace, and not of evil, to give you an expected end.

Psalm 30:5 (KJV) says, "For his anger endureth but a moment; in his favour is life: weeping may endure for a night, but joy cometh in the morning."

Phillipians 4:7 (KJV) says, "And the peace of God, which passeth all understanding, shall keep your hearts and minds through Christ Jesus.

Isaiah 25:4 says, "For thou hast been a strength to the poor, a strength to the needy in his distress, a refuge from the storm, a shadow from the heat, when the blast of the terrible ones is as a storm against the wall."

II Samuel 22:33 (KJV) says, "God is my strength and power: and he maketh my way perfect."

I don't know about you, but just reflecting over those scriptures give me hope and confidence that I will survive. Not only does He want you to survive, He wants you to prosper after you come out of it.

God is concerned even about the little things after He has delivered you. Do you remember the massive manhunt Pharoah had out against the children of Israel that caused the Lord to have to part the Red Sea? Let me refresh your memory so that I might bring up a point that should make your spirit shout.

Exodus 14: 8:22 (KJV) says, "And the LORD hardened the heart of Pharaoh King of Egypt, and he pursued after the children of Israel: and the children of Israel went out with an high hand. But the Egyptians pursued after them, all the horses and chariots of Pharaoh, and his horsemen, and his army, and overtook them encamping by the sea, beside Pihahiroth, before Baalzephon. And when Pharaoh drew nigh, the children of Israel lifted up their eyes, and, behold, the Egyptians marched after them; and they were sore afraid: and the children of Israel cried out unto the LORD. And they said unto Moses, Because there were no graves in Egypt, hast thou taken us away to die in the wilderness? wherefore hast thou dealt thus with us, to carry us forth out of Egypt? Is not this the word that we did tell thee in Egypt, saying, Let us alone, that we may serve the Egyptians? For it had been better for us to serve the Egyptians, than that we should die in the wilderness. And Moses said unto the people, Fear ye not, stand still, and see the salvation of the LORD, which he will shew to you to day: for the

Egyptians whom ye have seen today, ye shall see them again no more forever. The LORD shall fight for you, and ye shall hold your peace. And the LORD said unto Moses, Wherefore criest thou unto me? Speak unto the children of Israel, that they go forward: But lift thou up thy rod, and stretch out thine hand over the sea, and divide it: and the children of Israel shall go on dry ground through the midst of the sea. And I, behold, I will harden the hearts of the Egyptians, and they shall follow them: and I will get me honour upon Pharaoh, and upon all his host, upon his chariots, and upon his horsemen. And the Egyptians shall know that I am the LORD, when I have gotten me honour upon Pharaoh, upon his chariots, and upon his horsemen. And the angel of God, which went before the camp of Israel, removed and went behind them; and the pillar of the cloud went from before their face, and stood behind them: And it came between the camp of the Egyptians and the camp of Israel; and it was a cloud and darkness to them, but it gave light by night to these: so that the one came not near the other all the night. And Moses stretched out his hand over the sea; and the LORD caused the sea to go back by a strong east wind all that night, and made the sea dry land, and the waters were divided. And the children of Israel went into the midst of the sea upon the dry ground: and the waters were a wall unto them on their right hand, and on their left.

I have always marveled at that miracle not only because He parted one of the deepest seas of the seas, but because He caused them to walk through on dry land. Dry land? Really? Do you see the dynamic in that? Just think about how long it takes a load of your clothes to dry after washing them. Water had covered the floor of the sea since its existence yet it became dry instantly. He not only delivered them, but He made the deliverance a little easy. Sure, they were running for their lives, but imagine trying to escape serial killers and your feet is getting stuck in the floor of the sea. Wow. How great is our God! He made the escape so simple that all they had to do was keep moving. They had to push through their fear, through their doubt, and embrace that their God was indeed a deliverer and KEEP IT MOVING!

Imagine if they had stopped. They had a certain timeframe to get through there or else they would have been drowned with Pharaoh's assailants.

Here's what you need to know.

Your survival can very well rest on your determination to keep going. When God gives you the way of escape, you have to take it. Not all the time will you be picked up out of your storm and placed over into your peace. Sometimes you have to make a move. Sometimes you might have to step outside of your comfort zone and make a run for it. Sometimes you may even have to leave some people behind. I don't know about you but I am willing to make whatever sacrifice I have to make in order to get peace in my life—as long as the peace comes.

I love the story of Joseph as it relates to this subject. He was placed in a pit by his brothers and was left to die with no way of getting out. But, he did get out. You know how the story goes. He survived the betrayal of his family, the challenging of his integrity with Potiphar's wife and much more, all to end up in the palace holding a well respected government official position. He had to get go through to get through. And, no matter what you have to go through, you will survive.

How can I be so sure you will make it? Because God loves you and He wants you to survive—and you WILL.

William A. Jordan

Chapter Nine

~

The Perfect Storm

And when it was determined that we should sail into Italy, they delivered Paul and certain other prisoners unto one named Julius, a centurion of Augustus' band. And entering into a ship of Adramyttium, we launched, meaning to sail by the coasts of Asia; one Aristarchus, a Macedonian of Thessalonica, being with us.And the next day we touched at Sidon. And Julius courteously entreated Paul, and gave him liberty to go unto his friends to refresh himself.

And when we had launched from thence, we sailed under Cyprus, because the winds were contrary. And when we had sailed over the sea of Cilicia and Pamphylia, we came to Myra, a city of Lycia. And there the centurion found a ship of Alexandria sailing into Italy; and he put us therein.

And when we had sailed slowly many days, and scarce were come over against Cnidus, the wind not suffering us, we sailed under Crete, over against Salmone; And, hardly passing it, came unto a place which is called The fair havens; nigh whereunto was the city of Lasea. Now when much time was spent, and when sailing was now dangerous, because the fast was now already past, Paul admonished them, and said unto them, Sirs, I perceive that this voyage will be with hurt and much damage, not only of the lading and ship, but also of our lives.

Nevertheless the centurion believed the master and the owner of the ship, more than those things which were spoken by Paul. And because the haven was not commodious to winter in, the more part advised to depart thence also, if by any means they might attain to Phenice, and there to winter; which is an haven of Crete, and lieth toward the south west and north west. And when the south wind blew softly, supposing that they had obtained their purpose, loosing thence, they sailed close by Crete.

But not long after there arose against it a tempestuous wind, called Euroclydon. And when the ship was caught, and could not bear up into the wind, we let her drive. And running under a certain island which is called Clauda, we had much work to come by the boat: Which when they had taken up, they used helps, undergirding the ship; and, fearing lest they should fall into the quicksands, strake sail, and so were driven. And we being exceedingly tossed with a tempest, the next day they lightened the ship; And the third day we cast out with our own hands the tackling of the ship.

And when neither sun nor stars in many days appeared, and no small tempest lay on us, all hope that we should be saved was then taken away. But after long abstinence Paul stood forth in the midst of them, and said, Sirs, ye should have hearkened unto me, and not have loosed from Crete, and to have gained this harm and loss.

And now I exhort you to be of good cheer: for there shall be no loss of any man's life among you, but of the ship. For there stood by me this night the angel of God, whose I am, and whom I serve, Saying, Fear not, Paul; thou must be brought before Caesar: and, lo, God hath given thee all them that sail with thee. Wherefore, sirs, be of good cheer: for I believe God, that it shall be even as it was told me. Howbeit we must be cast upon a certain island. But when the fourteenth night was come, as we were driven up and down in Adria, about midnight the shipmen deemed that they drew near to some country; And sounded, and found it twenty fathoms: and when they had gone a little further, they sounded again, and found it fifteen fathoms.

Then fearing lest we should have fallen upon rocks, they cast four anchors out of the stern, and wished for the day. And as the shipmen were about to flee out of the ship, when they had let down the boat into the sea, under colour as though they would have cast anchors out of the foreship,

Paul said to the centurion and to the soldiers, Except these abide in the ship, ye cannot be saved. Then the soldiers cut off the ropes of the boat, and let her fall off.

And while the day was coming on, Paul besought them all to take meat, saying, This day is the fourteenth day that ye have tarried and continued fasting, having taken nothing. Wherefore I pray you to take some meat: for this is for your health: for there shall not an hair fall from the head of any of you.

And when he had thus spoken, he took bread, and gave thanks to God in presence of them all: and when he had broken it, he began to eat. Then were they all of good cheer, and they also took some meat. And we were in all in the ship two hundred threescore and sixteen souls.

And when they had eaten enough, they lightened the ship, and cast out the wheat into the sea. And when it was day, they knew not the land: but they discovered a certain creek with a shore, into the which they were minded, if it were possible, to thrust in the ship.

And when they had taken up the anchors, they committed themselves unto the sea, and loosed the rudder bands, and hoised up the mainsail to the wind, and made toward shore. And falling into a place where two seas met, they ran the ship aground; and the forepart stuck fast, and

*remained unmoveable, but the hinder part was broken with
the violence of the waves. And the soldiers' counsel was to kill
the prisoners, lest any of them should swim out, and escape.
But the centurion, willing to save Paul, kept them from their
purpose; and commanded that they which could swim should
cast themselves first into the sea, and get to land: And the rest,
some on boards, and some on broken pieces of the ship. And so
it came to pass, that they escaped all safe to land.*

As good as the stories have been that I've opened
previous chapters with; I did not write that one above. That
is the King James Version of the Acts 27 text. Reads like an
excerpt from a novel, huh? It is often said that truth is
stranger than fiction, and in the case of the above story, I
must say that I concur.

I am sure you have heard many sermonic illustrations
using that text, and my objective is not to reveal some new,
amazing revelation about it, but instead remind you that
even in a storm that can be avoided; even in a storm with
people around you who are not like you; even in a storm that
seems it will never end...every storm will eventually pass
over.

First thing I want to note is Paul's warning. He tried to
warn them against going into storm, but who was he? He was
a prisoner. They ignored his warning possibly because of his
current state. We have already established in previous
chapters that some storms we bring on ourselves. Some
storms we can prevent just by obeying the voice of the one
who can foresee what is about to happen. How many times
have you been watching the weather report, and heard the
meteorologists warn of a storm system approaching, and
encourage everyone to get to safety? There has probably
been at least one occasion where you ignored the warning

because you really did not believe the storm would affect you?

I can bet you have been in a church service and your Pastor has issued warnings about some things you needed to change, a course you needed to detour from, or habits and practices you needed to forsake. The unfortunate thing about that is, sermons and messages of warning are often ignored if the listener does not feel it applies to them at that moment. But, I want to challenge you to pay close attention to those who have been given charge over your soul. Even if God sends a warning through someone else, take heed. The warnings don't always come through someone who "looks" like they hear from God, but take heed anyway.

The captain and owner of this ship in this story chose to ignore Paul's warning and they set out to sea. Be careful who you allow to influence you. You need to make sure you know how to hear God for yourself. God may speak something to you and no one else may understand your reason for being obedient, but be obedient anyway.

No sooner than they could get out on the water, a wind arose—possibly a hurricane—and they found themselves in danger. They perceived that the ship was too heavy and consequently, they started dumping things off of the ship. What is on your ship that needs to be tossed over? Is there something or someone weighing you down, preventing you from sailing effectively? I wonder how more effective you would be at managing your storms if you got rid of some things from your lives. Here is the kicker. Most of the things weighing us down don't even belong to us. It is the stress, the worries, and the pressures of other people. Get rid of it. Release it.

In verse twenty, the storm gets so bad; the Bible says all hope for survival was loss. This is the time when death began to plague their mind. This was the time when they tried to come to grips with the fact they would soon perish. It looked as if the storm had overpowered them. There was no Facebook or Twitter for them to post or tweet messages of love to their family and loved ones. They were so far out; smoke signals would not have done any good. In their mind, it was over. They were finished.

BUT...

A word came from God through Paul. The man of God gets up in the midst of them, reminds them that they should have heeded the warning, and proceeds to tell them they are going to make it. He said, you'll lose the ship, but you'll escape with your life. That has been my intent in writing this book. I want you to know you may lose a few material possessions, some loved ones may walk out of your life, but you WILL escape with your life. You are going to survive.

Paul says to them, "I believe God." And there it is. When you have a word from God, whose report will you believe when the circumstances don't match what He said?

I know the doctor may have given you a bad report, but believe God.

I know it looks as if your marriage won't be saved, but believe God.

I know your children are acting like offspring of the enemy, but believe God.

What has God said about your situation? What has He promised you? I don't care what happens or what it looks like; with everything in you, with everything coming at you, still stand on the Word of God. It never fails. His word is true. It is life.

Paul never announces when they would make it to safety, and fourteen days later, they were still battling the storm. Beloved, don't allow the tenure of your storm to make you doubt what God said. We discussed this earlier in the book. He may not come when you want Him, but He is coming.

So, as they kept sailing, some of the fellas decided they were going do it their way by dropping some small boats in an effort to escape. Paul steps up once again and offers a warning. He tells the people in charge that if the guys left the boat, they would all die. That leads me to say this. Do not deviate from the instructions of the Lord because you think you can handle things on your own. That will get you in trouble and can possibly mean your survival. Again, this is why you need to be able to hear when God is speaking to you even if He speaks to you through someone else. Don't try to do things your way. You do not have the power to sustain yourself.

On the fourteenth day, Paul admonishes them to do something practical. Eat. Remember in a previous chapter we talked about this. Not everything is deep. Often we drown in shallow water because we complicate things that really are very simple. He tells them to eat. He knew the storm was not going to end smoothly, and they would later have to swim to safety. What if they had not eaten? They would have lacked the strength to swim to shore. What would happen if you went on vacation and got recharged and rejuvenated? Would you feel like going on if you got some rest for a change?

Would you be able to endure if you took some time to regroup? Do not ever allow anyone to make you feel bad for resting. Anyone who knows me knows I will take me a day to myself—unapologetically. So what if they call you lazy? So what if they say bosses never sleep. Child, please. Get you a good meal and get some rest. Resting ain't never hurt nobody. The Bible tells us they were all in good cheer after they ate. Are you surprised? You know we have major attitudes when we don't eat anyway. Especially when we don't eat and are going through some trouble.

After everyone ate, they lightened the ship even more by tossing over the wheat, and soon after everyone had gotten full and were in a better mood, they spotted a bay with a nice beach. They decided it was a good place to run the ship onto land. But, they didn't make it. They hit a reef and the ship BROKE into pieces. For goodness sake, it seemed as if they couldn't catch a break!

Have you ever felt like you were so close to something but something else happens that prohibits you from making it? How frustrating it is to get close to a dream but have to walk away from it because another obstacle gets in your way?

These guys were going through it. After all the lightening of the ship they did to keep it from sinking, no one had even thought about it breaking. Yet, it had broken. The soldiers saw that it was possible for the prisoners to escape, and sought to kill them, but the man of God was on the ship. The centurion wanted to save Paul and by saving Paul, the others were saved as well. That's why it's important to know who you are surrounded by. You need to make sure you are connected to some people who have the favor of God on their life.

Well, the story goes on to let us know that they ship broke into pieces within a distance that was close enough for them to swim to land. My brothers and sisters, it may take a little more work, but be determined. Be determined that you are not going to get to that close to the finish line and give up. The preacher, the pagan, and the prisoners were commanded to swim. For those who could not swim, they got on boards, and some swam in on broken pieces.

Here it is.

I don't care how you get there, just GET THERE! No matter your method for surviving the storm, just survive it. But, I urge you, don't give up at the sign of a little more trouble. Keep on swimming. Keep on floating. Don't survive the storm and then give up after it is over simply because you are not hand delivered the promise. Don't survive depression and oppression for all these years, and then let the storm you're in now, take you out.

Some of them were on boards and some on broken pieces meant there was enough provision for everybody to have what they needed to survive. Some had the ability to swim, others didn't. The point? Don't be worried about how your neighbor is getting to safety; you just do what YOU can.

No storm can last forever. They must all come to PASS. They will all end and just on the other side of it is a bright and sunny day.

Just as Paul prophesied their survival in this text, I want to end this book by telling you that you, too, have a promise. God's plan for you is perfect, and whether you are in a storm to learn something or whether you are in a storm because you brought it upon yourself; you WILL survive.

Beloved, the truth of the matter is, you have *already* survived.

Pastor William Anthony Jordan is the Founder of W.A.J. Ministries. He serves as the Senior Pastor of Lyons Unity Missionary Baptist Church in Houston, Texas.

Pastor Jordan received his Bachelor of Theology degree and was conferred with his Master of Theology Degree on November 8, 2005 both from the Slidell Baptist Seminary.

Pastor Jordan is a member of Brentwood Baptist Church located in Houston, TX under the leadership of Rev. Dr. Joe Samuel Ratliff. Because of God's Grace, He is empowered to reach the lost at any cost, by continuing to preach and teach the Word of God in order to exalt the Savior, evangelize the sinner, equip the saved and edify the saints!

WAJ Ministries was birthed in order to expand Pastor Jordan's commitment to service and mentoring other leaders. As he travels the country ministering the Word of God, he has become a leader's leader, leveraging WAJ Ministries to tap into his gifts and help others develop the principles it takes to survive and serve in excellence.

Having authored his first book, Storm Survivors, slated for release in January 2013. His power-filled, impactful messages are sure to be the "How to" for ministries and leadership training around the world.

Pastor William Anthony Jordan is married to Nikki Ellis Jordan and they have been blessed with one son, Jeff Taylor and one daughter, Amiya Elizabeth, who are all active in the Kingdom of God.